T0253349

STEEL of the CELESTIAL SHADOWS 3

STORY & ART

DARUMA MATSUURA

SUPERVISION BY
TOSHIKI MIZUTANI
NOBORU HISAYAMA

MADARA   AKI   TSUKI   RYUDO KONOSUKE

A woman shunned by society for her ability. She stands in the way of Konosuke and Aki.

A bright and cheery traveling *ichiko* medium. She's arrived in Edo for reasons of her own.

An otherworldly beauty who mysteriously appeared from nowhere to wed Konosuke. Why does she adore him so?

A low-ranking samurai who can't seem to catch a break. Metal warps when he touches it or it gets near his body, so he can't wield a blade.

Ryudo Konosuke is a low-ranking samurai struggling to survive abject poverty. He owes his destitution to his seemingly cursed ability to warp any metal that comes near him. One day, a beautiful woman named Tsuki shows up at Konosuke's door and marries him. Their happiness is short-lived, however, as Tsuki is whisked away by a strange man with supernatural powers. When Aki—a blind medium with the ability to view a person's future—finds her way to Konosuke, he is determined to use his new friend's power to save Tsuki. But there are dark forces conspiring against him...

[CONTENTS]

18   Heliosphere   5

19   Butterfly Diagram   25

20   Plage   47

21   Heliopause   67

22   Spicule   89

23   Rim   109

24   Analemma   131

25   Photosphere   151

26   Corona Hole   171

JUST GET RID OF THIS MANZAI GANG!

CHAPTER 18
◎
HELIOSPHERE

TSUKI... HELPED YOUR MOTHER?

WHAT? NAH, IT WASN'T HER. NEVER MIND, FOR NOW...

SHK

UGH ...

WHY DID YOU STEAL TSUKI AWAY?!

AND ON WHOSE ORDERS?

A-ALL WE WERE TOLD WAS...

BAM PAH

A-ANOTHER ONE!

SOUNDS LIKE A KID?

RUN! RUN!

THMP THMP THMP THMP

IS YOUR ENTRYWAY THROUGH THIS DOOR?!

LET ME OPEN IT!

W-WAIT!

HUH?!

...

Ack!

Whoa!

THAT'S WHERE OTOKICHI LOST HIS LIFE!

K·A·K·K

CROWS!

ON MAYURA KIRANDI SOWAKA...

CROWS?

I HAVE A SOFT SPOT...

...FOR FELLOW ICHIKO.

I'M LETTING YOU LIVE, SO GET OUT OF HERE!

HUH?! WHY?!

I'M A HEARTH EXORCIST, YOU SEE...

HUH?!

PICKING ON *HIM*, YOU SAY?

LET ME TELL YOU ABOUT SAMURAI.

WHY'S EVERYONE SO KEEN ON PICKING ON THIS SAMURAI?!

FIRST THE MURDEROUS MANZAI, NOW YOU FOLKS...

SINCE THEY CONTROL THE PERMITS, YOU MIGHT CALL 'EM THE FIRST FAMILY OF ONMYODO.

THEY UNIFIED FORTUNE TELLERS AND DIVINERS 'ROUND THE NATION, STARTING WITH THE ONMYOJI.

...ARE DIRECT DESCENDANTS OF **ABE-NO-SEIMEI**, THE LEGENDARY ONMYOJI.

WHICH KINDA MAKES SENSE, BECAUSE GENERATIONS OF THEIR CLAN HEADS...

WELL...

SEE...

INCLUDING THAT MANZAI TROUPE AND THAT PAIR OF ASCETICS?

ONMYOJI? REAL SORCERERS?

WORD IS, THOSE FORTUNE TELLERS THEY MANAGE ARE JUST A FRONT FOR WHAT'S REALLY GOING ON.

THERE'S RUMORS ABOUT THE TSUCHIMIKADO CLAN.

...TAKE THEIR MARCHING ORDERS FROM THAT CLAN.

IN TRUTH, MOST OF THE GIFTED ACROSS JAPAN...

"G..."

They move...

...

"GIFTED," YOU SAY?

...but not in the street. Somewhere out of sight!

Eliminate them...

...toward Senju.

...THEY'LL BE PASSING BY KOZUKAPPARA...

HYOGO-SAMA.

SOUNDS LIKE...

STEEL *of the*
CELESTIAL
SHADOWS

Trivia of the Celestial Shadows

#①

- Divided into *wakado* (footman), *chugen* (attendant), and *komono* (lowliest servant).
- When a samurai reported to the castle for work, he would be accompanied by several such servants.

- The number of servants varied depending on family status and wealth. One might have two servants for every 100 koku of rice produced in a year (the koku being the standard measure of wealth at the time).

- However, many examples of *ukiyo-e* art portray a single samurai walking about with a single servant.

- A samurai unaccompanied by any servants while out and about would raise suspicions (at worst, the authorities might be alerted).

- Some servants worked for the same family for decades, while others might have been temps hired through an employment agency (Otokichi was the former type).

Hasami-bako traveling chest

Samurai Family's Hokonin Man-servants

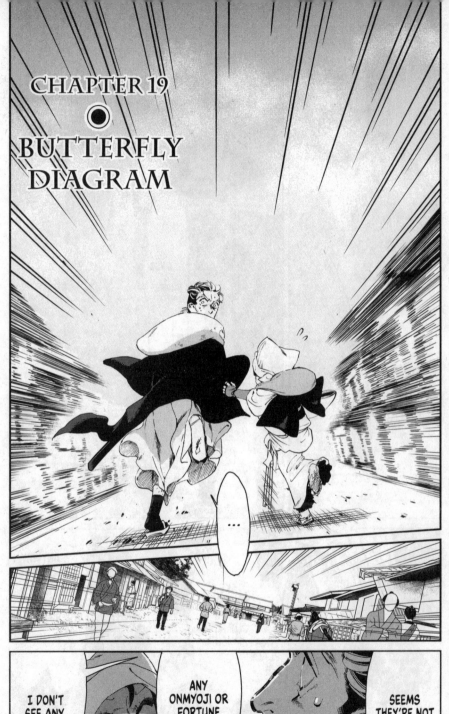

CHAPTER 19
⬤
BUTTERFLY DIAGRAM

...

I DON'T SEE ANY.

ANY ONMYOJI OR FORTUNE TELLERS AROUND?

SEEMS THEY'RE NOT FOLLOWING US.

YOU DO KNOW WHY THIS PLACE STINKS SO BAD, RIGHT?

WE'RE AT THE KOZUKAPPARA EXECUTION GROUNDS.

R-RIGHT.

WOULD YOU... MOURN THESE FOLKS?

PLEASE...

HMM?

YOU THERE.

THE ICHIKO.

YOU WANT ME TO PRAY FOR 'EM?

SURE THING.

YES.

W-WHAT?!

WHY PRAY FOR THE SOULS OF **CRIMINALS?**

WE'RE ALL EQUAL IN DEATH, SIR.

WELL, YES, BUT I MEAN...

MUCH APPRECI-ATED.

...

GOTTA FEEL BAD FOR THESE FELLAS.

...TO BE LAID BARE LIKE THIS, FOR PUBLIC SHAMING?

GUILTY OR NOT...

...GNAW AWAY AT THEIR CORPSES, RETURNING 'EM TO THE EARTH.

BUT AT LEAST THE INSECTS...

DON'T YOU THINK...

WE ALL TURN TO DIRT, HELPING THE GRASS, THE FLOWERS, AND THE BUGS TO LIVE THEIR BEST LIVES...

MAN OR WOMAN...

WHETHER GOOD OR EVIL...

...THERE'S SOMETHING *SUBLIME* ABOUT ALL THAT!

I'M GUESSIN'... YOU'RE NOT KIN OF THE DEPARTED?

...

SHNR

...BUT ANY LOWLY ICHIKO WHO STANDS AGAINST TSUCHIMIKADO-SAMA IS IN FOR A LOT MORE PAIN AND SUFFERING!

NOW I CAN'T RIGHTLY SAY WHY YOU'RE OUT HERE HELPING THE SAMURAI...

AND WHAT'S THAT STONE BLADE S'POSED TO DO?

BZZ
BZZ

ZZ

URK?!

HA
HA
HA
HA
HA
HA
HA

I...

...CAN'T
SEE!

REST
EASY.

YOU
FOLKS'LL
BE DIRT
SOON TOO.

BUT A WHOLE *SWARM*...

...AMOUNTS TO A MIGHTY BEAST.

A SINGLE BUG'S NO GREAT THREAT...

...IS MORE THAN ENOUGH...

AND THE POISON FROM A SWARM OF BLISTER BEETLES...

...TO KILL A GROWN MAN.

ONCE THEY CRAWL INSIDE YOU, THAT IS.

UGH...

FWAP

SPUT

POP

?!

SQUISH 'EM, AND THEIR JUICE'LL SHOW YOU A NEW WORLD OF PAIN...

HEH HEH.

THAT ONE? THAT'S A ROVE BEETLE.

LOTTA DIFFERENT KINDS GOT INTO THAT SWARM.

YOU'LL NEVER MANAGE TO SWAT AWAY JUST THE BLISTER BEETLES.

HECK, THEY'LL CRAWL INTO YOUR EYE SOCKETS.

OR EVEN YOUR EARS!

COVER YOUR MOUTH, AND THEY'LL FIND YOUR NOSE.

WHP

WHP

FWMP

BZZ

BZZ

BZZ

OWW...

DAMN!

HFF

HFF

STEEL *of the* CELESTIAL SHADOWS

Trivia of the Celestial Shadows #②

Goze Buskers

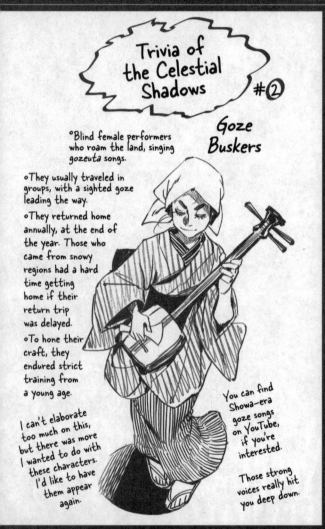

°Blind female performers who roam the land, singing gozeuta songs.

○They usually traveled in groups, with a sighted goze leading the way.

○They returned home annually, at the end of the year. Those who came from snowy regions had a hard time getting home if their return trip was delayed.

○To hone their craft, they endured strict training from a young age.

I can't elaborate too much on this, but there was more I wanted to do with these characters. I'd like to have them appear again.

You can find Showa-era goze songs on YouTube, if you're interested.

Those strong voices really hit you deep down.

DAMNED BUGS.

IF ONLY...

...THEY DIDN'T SPRING OUTTA ME LIKE THAT.

...

HFF

HFF

HFF

CHAPTER 21 ◎ HELIOPAUSE

TURN
AROUND
AND RUN
ABOUT FIVE
KEN!*

ICHIKO-
DONO!

STEEL of the CELESTIAL SHADOWS

Trivia of the Celestial Shadows #③

Manzai Performer

o Around the New Year, they traveled around, putting on celebratory performances.

o Usually a two-person team, with one playing the Tayu role and the other the Saizo role.

o Since they could trace their roots back to the shomoji performers (lower class, civilian onmyoji) of the middle ages, at least in some regions, they wound up falling under control of the Tsuchimikado Clan, which oversaw all onmyoji in the early modern period (Azuchi-Momoyama to the end of the Edo Period).

° The origin of modern-day manzai comedy performances.

I'm the Tayu here!

The manzai practiced in modern times (like Mikawa-style manzai) involves performances that even people nowadays find delightful!

I hope these traditions stick around for a long time.

CHAPTER 22
SPICULE

"PLEASE."

"KEEP ON..."

"...LIVING."

MY TSUKI...

...WILL DIE?

TSUKI...

...WILL BE KILLED?

HFF

HFF

THEY SAID BLADES **WOULDN'T WORK** ON HIM...

...WITHOUT EVEN TOUCHING IT!

HE'S MANIPULATING THAT GIANT KHAKKHARA STAFF...

...BUT HIS GIFT'S MORE THAN JUST THAT...

...AN
AWAKEN-
ING?

HM?

OH NO.
DID HE
ACHIEVE...

THANKS
...

LITTLE
ONES...

STOPPING
THE
BLEEDING
FOR ME?

URGH!!

KLAT
KLAT
KLATR
KLATR

RATTL
RATTL

SIR!

HEY!

DO
YOU
HEAR
ME?

KNK
BNK

KA
KA
KI

GNAL

KLAT
KLAT
KLAT

KLAT

KLAT

KLAT

THE
BLOODLUST IS
THE ONLY THING
KEEPING HIM
GOING...

HE CAN'T
HEAR A
WORD...

HFF HFF HFF

THEY... FEAR HIM?!

...ARE STAYING AWAY?

THE BUGS...

...HIMSELF
AGAIN...

STEEL *of the* CELESTIAL SHADOWS

Trivia of the Celestial Shadows

#④

Ichiko Mediums

∘A.K.A. *miko.* They were different in a number of ways from the miko maidens employed by shrines in modern times.

∘There were also ichiko/miko who lived at specific shrines (as priests' wives, for instance), but plenty of ichiko traveled around making a living by performing seances or reading fortunes, like Aki. Another type worked as prostitutes.

∘The word differed from region to region. They were called azasamiko, *ichiko, itako, nonou* (in Shinano), *onakate* (in Yamagata), *shiroyumoji, itaka, kongarasate,* and so on.

∘Many would carry around gehobako boxes full of tools.

∘Ichiko never had a central organization, the way onmyoji and Shugendo practitioners did. They would defer to their husbands, fathers, or foster fathers.

∘Many would end up marrying religious figures such as onmyoji or Shugendo practitioners.

Note

✗ There were also royal court ichiko, but I'm only writing about civilian ichiko here.

I took creative liberties with Aki's outfit. It's not historically accurate.

TSUKI
...

TSUKI?!

I SWEAR I HEARD...

...YOUR VOICE...

FMP

CHAPTER 24
● ANALEMMA

Ugh...

SLMP

ICHIKO-DONO?!

BWAH

GAAH

SO NOW...

...IT'S SPIDERS?!

HUH?

SKTTR
SKTTR

IS THAT...

...HER ARM?

DID I SEVER IT?!

M...

ME, OF ALL PEOPLE ?!

MAYBE ...

I CAN'T EVEN HOLD ONE!

NO!

...WITH A KATANA?

FROM BIRTH, I'VE NEVER BEEN ABLE...

...TO TOUCH A SWORD, NOR ANY METAL...

AND ANY ATTEMPT TO DO SO...

...ALWAYS ENDS WITH...

TAP

SIR?

MM, SURE...

...

MUCH LIKE THAT IRON NAIL YOU HOLD...

...THE METAL WARPING ITSELF TO REJECT ME.

CAN'T HAVE BEEN EASY FOR YOU, SIR.

A SAMURAI WITH A GIFT LIKE THAT?

A GIFT?

AND YOUR ABILITY...

A SPECIAL POWER, SIR.

YES.

WANNA TRY IT OUT?

...GIVES ME AN IDEA.

HE'S TOO MUCH...

DAMN ...

...WITH A GIFT LIKE THAT...

...HE'LL THREATEN HARETAKE-SAMA'S ULTIMATE DREAM!

BUT IF I LET HIM GET AWAY...

...HARETAKE-SAMA!

I WON'T LET HIM SCREW IT ALL UP...

...BEATEN TO DEATH OR WORSE IN THAT BACKWATER SHITHOLE OF A TEMPLE!

...I WOULD'VE BEEN...

IF YOU HADN'T LIFTED ME OUT OF MY MISERABLE LIFE...

"...BE BUMPED OFF TOO!"

BW

RM

KINK CHAK KLAK

WELL?

TH-THEY MOVED!

BUT...

...LIKE THEY HAD MINDS OF THEIR OWN...

B ZZ

BA M

THE BUG WOMAN'S BACK!

BZZ

IT'S HER!

B... BEES?!

BZZ

CAN YOU DO LIKE I TOLD YOU?

SIR!

BUT...

I GOTTA TRY!

I...

...DON'T KNOW!

BZZ

MRGH?!

BZZ

BZZ

BZZ

...MERE BEES SHOULD BE...

Damn!

AFTER TOXIC BEETLES AND LOCUSTS...

TSUKI!

I WON'T LET THEM END YOU!

YOU ARE MINE...

HARE-TAKE-SAMA...

I DON'T MATTER MUCH...

BUT YOUR DREAM'S GOTTA LIVE ON...

BNG

...TO PROTECT!

STEEL *of the* CELESTIAL SHADOWS

Trivia of the Celestial Shadows

⑤

Kozukappara Execution Grounds

> Even at night, it's a bright, clean train station area (I took a stroll)

o Located near Minami–Senju Station these days.

o Travelers entering Edo via Senju would have to pass by. This was intentional; they *had* to bear witness.

An Enmei Jizo statue was built here in memoriam of the condemned and executed. It still exists today, though it's known as the Kubikiri Jizo (decapitation Jizo).

o In the Bakumatsu period, samurai would casually suggest a visit to the execution grounds, as if on a dare.

o There was apparently a red-light district nearby. I'd expect there to be some spooky songs about the execution grounds from that period, but nothing turned up in my research. Maybe you'll have more luck searching?

Crucifix

Severed heads on display

Guard house

← To Sanya, Yoshiwara

Passing travelers

→ To Senjuohashi

CHAPTER 25

⬤

PHOTOSPHERE

...FIGURE OUT...

...I WILL...

...HOW TO CONTROL METAL!

WHAT HE CAN'T DO...

...IS LOSE HIMSELF TO ANGER, LIKE BEFORE!

....

...THERE SHOULD BE A WAY.

EVEN WITHOUT RAGE OR A GRUDGE POWERING HIM...

...AND INSPIRE HIM TO NEVER SURRENDER...

A WAY TO GIVE HIS HEART A GOOD SHAKING...

AN EMOTION.

I YEARN TO FEEL YOU.

TSUKI...

THERE IS NO OTHER PATH.

...BY YOUR SIDE.

TO LIVE...

...LIGHT TO THE FUTURE.

YOU ARE MY ONE AND ONLY...

YOU SPOKE THOSE WORDS TO ME...

...BUT RIGHT NOW...

"EVEN WITHOUT A BLADE OF STEEL."

...

I HAVE NEED.

ESPECIALLY NOW...

NOR FOR MY MOTHER'S SAKE!

NOT AS PROOF THAT I AM SAMURAI!

...BUT I'VE NO IDEA WHERE SHE IS...

HFF

HFF

I MADE THE NAIL MOVE...

GRP

FWAP

EVEN SO!

I OPEN...

...A PATH TO THE FUTURE.

STEEL of the CELESTIAL SHADOWS

Madara Concept Art

Madara

Wields bugs. Strictly speaking, she summons them from else-where.

Views herself and the bugs as one and the same.

Born in a rural community, she emerged from her mother covered in insects. Later, a poor harvest (caused by leafhopper bugs) was blamed on her. The townsfolk decided to burn her, in the fashion of the traditional torch procession to purge crop-eating bugs. After barely escaping with her life, she was taken in by a temple. While assisting grave diggers on the temple grounds, she could avoid prying eyes.

Haretake made her aware of the value of her own life, and of the lives of bugs. She came to believe that bugs, humans, and all of nature are essential elements of the world. Because Haretake is such an absolute figure to her, she's more than willing to kill those who might threaten him. By viewing all life as being equally valuable (to an extreme extent), she doesn't think highly of any given individual life.

Insect aficionado Shiba Kokan once said, "I feel that humans and insects are not so fundamentally different."

RELAX.

...AND OUT.

HAAH

FWOO

NICE AND SLOW. BREATHE IN...

HFFF

CALM DOWN.

CAN YOU GET UP? LEAN ON MY SHOULDER.

OL' RYUDO'S JUST FINE.

HEY! BOKU-
TAKE!

PICK UP THE PACE, OR THEY'LL BE ON OUR TAIL!

RIGHT!

I'M BOKUTAKE!

WHO... ARE THESE PEOPLE?

AND OVER THERE'S MY PAL, ZANNEN.

YOU'LL WANNA CLEAR YOUR HEAD OF ALL THOUGHTS WHEN BOKUTAKE'S NEAR.

HOW'D HE KNOW MY NAME?

HE'S GOT A TALENT FOR READING MINDS.

WE'RE NO STRANGERS TO OL' RYUDO.

Y'GOT THAT, AKI-SAN?

A SHORTCUT, COURTESY OF A HEX.

EVERY INARI SHRINE ACROSS EDO CONNECTS TO THIS PASSAGE.

FWOOOOOO

NOT ME. THIS'S COURTESY OF MY *MASTER.*

YUP!

...HIS GIFT'S NOT BEHIND THIS...

BUT...

TUG TUG

BOKU-TAKE!!

MY MASTER'S WAY MORE DASHING. SMARTER, TOO.

ZANNEN AIN'T MY MASTER, IF YOU'RE WONDERING.

AH.

...ARE ALL AGENTS OF THE TSUCHI-MIKADO.

...AND THAT MADARA GAL WHO YOUR PAL TOOK OUT...

SO ZANNEN, ME...

BUT...

TH-THEY'RE ALLIED WITH THE BUG LADY?!

TSUKI-SAN...

THIS FELLA'S WIFE SAVED MY HIDE ONCE.

...

KLAT

*THE SUMIDA RIVER

...AND WILL LEAVE EDO BY BOAT.

NOW WE'VE HIT THE OKAWA*...

Y'KNOW THE OHASHI BRIDGE? WE CROSSED TO THE OTHER SHORE, TO HASHIDO INARI SHRINE.

W-WHERE ARE WE?

KLAK

TMP

TMP

KLAK

AKI.

SORRY I CAN'T HELP YA DOWN!

WATCH YOUR STEP!

"OUR EYES..."

"...MAY NOT SEE THE LIGHT."

"HOWEVER..."

CARE-FUL!

WOBBL

[**WITH HELP FROM**]

(in no particular order,
and with titles omitted)

My Staff

Saburo Kirigakure

Doom Kobayashi

Masashi Motegi (Tadashi Sato)

Satoko Matsumoto

Hiroto Yokoyama

Subaru Niina

Takanashi

Fuki Hinohara

Saki Toda

Daichi Kawada

[**CONSULTANTS**]

Noboru Hisayama

Toshiki Mizutani

[**ORIGINAL DESIGN**]

Kohei Nawata Design Office

[**RESEARCH ASSISTANCE**]

Kazuya Namiki
  [Jikishinkage-ryu Kuunkai]

Akira Takemoto

Bonus Comic

"Get readin', you."

I can't keep up with all the reading, but man—samurai and onmyoji are just so fascinating.

The Tsuchimikado Clan too.

I always had an interest in the culture and customs of the Edo period, and I was determined to create a historical fiction manga. Even doing the research is fun!

Everyone's looking worse for wear. Are they gonna be okay? Do they need a breather?

What's the next big threat waiting for these two, once their journey really begins?!

Even I didn't expect them to be battling for their lives before even stepping foot out of Edo.

BZZ

Look forward to volume 4!

Thanks for your continued support

END

STEEL *of the* CELESTIAL SHADOWS

Volume 3 • VIZ Signature Edition

Story & Art by **DARUMA MATSUURA**

Daruma Matsuura was born in 1984 in Kanagawa prefecture. Her debut series, *Kasane*, was serialized in 2013 and made into a live-action film in 2018. Other works include *Imakako* and *Utakata to Tomoshibi*. *Steel of the Celestial Shadows* is currently serialized in *Big Comic Superior* from Shogakukan. Her favorite sushi is uni.

TRANSLATION Caleb Cook
TOUCH-UP ART & LETTERING Steve Dutro
DESIGN Shawn Carrico
EDITOR Mike Montesa

TAIYO TO TSUKI NO HAGANE Vol. 3
by Daruma MATSUURA
© 2020 Daruma MATSUURA
All rights reserved.
Original Japanese edition published by SHOGAKUKAN. English translation rights in the United States of America, Canada, the United Kingdom, Ireland, Australia, and New Zealand arranged with SHOGAKUKAN.

SUPERVISION BY Toshiki MIZUTANI/Noboru HISAYAMA
ORIGINAL COVER DESIGN Kohei Nawata Design Office

The stories, characters, and incidents mentioned in this publication are entirely fictional.

No portion of this book may be reproduced or transmitted in any form or by any means without written permission from the copyright holders.

Printed in Canada

Published by VIZ Media, LLC
P.O. Box 77010
San Francisco, CA 94107

10 9 8 7 6 5 4 3 2 1
First printing, July 2024

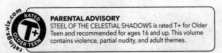
PARENTAL ADVISORY
STEEL OF THE CELESTIAL SHADOWS is rated T+ for Older Teen and recommended for ages 16 and up. This volume contains violence, partial nudity, and adult themes.

VIZ SIGNATURE
vizsignature.com